Your Cleaner Hates You

and other poems

Soulful Group

This edition was published by the Soulful Group in 2019

@soulfulgroup
www.soulfulgroup.com
we unlace words & detangle life

ISBN: 978-1-9998104-1-2

This collection is dedicated to two of the best
friends a woman could have, Paul Butler and Kirsty
Helliar.

Paul, almost everything I know that is interesting,
beautiful or just plain strange is because you have
always generously shared your learning and
thoughts with me and I'm beyond grateful to have
my own private curator of music, art, big ideas and
everything else. Thank you.

Kirsty, what can I say, partner in crime, partner in
rhyme and best poetry bitch ever. You have,
perhaps foolishly, joined in with far too many mad
plans and projects and mostly enjoyed them. You
make my world a better place and I'm forever
happy that you're here.

Thanks to Shobana Patel and everyone at the Soulful Group, without you, this book wouldn't exist.

Thanks to Wayne Mitchelson for exactly the cover design and artwork I envisaged.

To Lydia Towsey and Joelle Taylor, far better poets than me, thank you both for kindness above and beyond.

Thank you to the splendid Fran Bass whose bass artistry has added a whole other layer of skill to my definitely less talented writing.

I owe a debt of gratitude to all the spoken word promoters and performers without whom there would be no spoken word scene, thank you to all of you who have allowed me to perform or who have shared work that reminds me just how powerful poetry can be.

[1] Your Cleaner Hates You

Your Cleaner Hates You

Your cleaner hates you.

Not of course in the way she hates Crocs, Jacob
Rees Mogg or the kind of people who talk about
going for a cheeky Nando's,

But, make no mistake, your cleaner hates you.

And just because she knows the names of your
dog, guinea pigs and husband and remembers to
ask about your son, studying what was it ?...
forensic physiology and photography...don't be
fooled, your cleaner hates you.

Sometimes, your cleaner wonders what exactly it is
you do all day, given that you have a woman to
clean your house and a woman to iron your clothes
and another, slightly younger posher woman to
walk your dog...

Oh, they hate you too.

You tell your cleaner that you have 'projects' on the
go as you waft to your study on the 3rd floor, your
room of one's own.

What you don't do up there...ever...is bring down
the multitude of mouldy and malodorous mugs,
some homage to a long-gone undergraduate
lifestyle and your cleaner would like you to know

that emptying an ashtray into a wicker wastepaper
basket is exactly the same as not emptying it all but
with additional hoovering work.

Your cleaner hates you.

Your cleaner has flicked through your expensive
moleskin bound journal and quite frankly her
advice would be to not give up your day job, if of
course you had a day job to give up.

Your cleaner hates your poetry.

Your cleaner hates the rumpled crumpled used
tissues you leave in your unmade bed.

She hates the ring of pubic pelt around your bath,
but at least she knows for sure that you're not a
natural blonde.

But most of all your cleaner hates the notes:

The – *"House in a bit of a state today, please work your
usual magic, kiss kiss"*

The – *"If you get time today, can you empty all the kitchen
cupboards, clean them and put everything back, but you
know, just better, kiss, kiss, kiss"*

The – *"Don't bother coming for the next 2 weeks, we're
away, kiss"*

Come the glorious revolution, you will find yourself
not with your back against the wall, instead, you
will be issued with an official cleaner car, ancient,
prone to make noises so terrifyingly potentially
expensive that you will be forced to drive
everywhere with the stereo cranked up as loud as
you can bear, while you mumble prayers
to some god of pauper's transportation.

"Please just let the car last a few more months…"

And you will get to wear cleaner clothes, badly
fitting grey joggers and a sweatshirt full of holes
where neat bleach has burnt through fabric to meet
soft bare flesh.

Then, then you will become your cleaner's cleaner.

And your cleaner, your ex cleaner will look you in
the eye and she will know that you hate her, but
actually, actually, your cleaner, your ex cleaner, well
actually…

Your ex cleaner won't give a flying fuck.

There Is More To That Cleaner Than Meets The Eye

There is more to that cleaner than meets the eye…

This one gets up at five
Runs as fast and far as lungs and heart can bear
Revels in the recognition of other early morning
pavement pounders
Then puts on the uniform of tabard, bleach stained
leggings
Becomes invisible again

This one knows the name of every star that's in
the sky
And more than that can tell you why they are so
named
But has spent so long on hands and knees
She fears she may have lost the knack of
looking up

This one's boyfriend is banged up again
Working double shifts
She has curated a collection of childcare
So complicated, so tenuous
That in a gallery would be labelled web
Or DNA of everyday

This one says she's lucky
In a refugee camp far away
At 15,16
The soldiers felt she was too old to rape
So, mostly, she was left alone

This one speaks 5 languages
Including yours
So, knows exactly what your husband and his mates
make of her arse
When she bends down to scrub your skirting
boards
Laser jets from lowered lids
If looks could kill

This one holds a broken bird
A touch so light
It's as if her hands were wings
And not these red and swollen things
Fingerprints burnt off by bleach
Convenient she always thinks
Should she start a new career
As master thief

And this one
This one's writing poetry
Verse as vicious as vipers
Mouth so acidic it makes diamonds bleed
This one's writing poetry

There's more to that cleaner than you can ever see.

16 And A Bit Reasons To Be Nice To Your Cleaner

1. She knows what lives behind your sofa.

2. She knows what goes on behind closed doors.

3. She could, if she wanted to, clean your toilet with your toothbrush. She doesn't, but she could.

4. She knows you wear the same pyjamas for a week, or is it two ?

5. She knows who takes anti-depressants and who should, really, really should.

6. She could, if she wanted to, rewrite your magnetic fridge poetry into a rant of Polish obscenities, she could, but actually she doesn't have the time.

7. She knows whose son is drinking cider and whose son is dealing weed.

8. She knows whose daughter keeps a razor blade in a tiny tin under an almost still fluffy gnarled greying Bunnykins.

9. She could stop for a moment and think about what it would be like to sit at a scrubbed (by her, of course) pine table with Pilates pals and eat lemon drizzle cake, she could, but she knows that you monitor the hoover as it trundles from room to room, so she could, but she daren't.

10. She knows you didn't make the lemon drizzle cake.

11. She knows you did eat 3 packets of crisps, 2 large mars bars and a gluten free chocolate cake in bed this week.

12. She could tell you that her children got far better A-level results than yours, but she won't. She guards her privacy, the knowing and the knowledge is one-way street.

13. She knows you are £234.57 overdrawn one day after payday.

14. She knows that you shop in Aldi now, but carry it home in your Cath Kidston jute shopping bags.

15. She could make a fuss about the underpayment, the *didn't have any change*, the *will sort it out next week*, but she won't. Instead, she has taken to letting the Hoover run on, unminded, while she stares out of the windows, stealing back time.

16. She knows it won't be long now until you are the one picking up your husband's toenail clippings from the bedside table, scrubbing your own pine table, washing the plates your children leave under beds until they fester, become concrete, difficult to clean and then when she meets you, in the street, sometime next week, next year, maybe,
Your ex cleaner, well, she will be very nice to you indeed.

[2] Dogs...And People

I've Got Nothing Against Dogs Per Se,
She Says

The moment the words are out of her mouth, she wishes she hadn't said them.

they hang in the air, too heavy for their actual content, she particularly regrets the Latin tag, what was she thinking of ?

there is a pause, she sips her latte, extra shot, two sugars and wonders how to get this conversation back on track.

and now from no-where, she is actually impersonating the talking pug from you tube *"iiiiaaaaaa wuubbbbb yooooouuuuu"* - she even manages the little howl at the end.

there is another pause.

"I mean, - it's not like they talk very well or anything"

her daughter stares at her - torn midway between horror and her default position of mild derision for the mother who never ever gets it.

they both look down at their cake plates.

the mother cannot stop herself –

"it would be so much better if they said something interesting"

the daughter buries herself in her iPod playlist, she is prepared to give her mother half an ear, usually that's enough to avoid accusations of rudeness, the litany about the youth of today, but also ensures that she doesn't really have to pay any attention.

there is another pause, the mother says she wants to take the daughters' photo, but the girl hides her face in her jacket, refuses to pose.

there is a longer pause and then defeated, she puts the camera away.

"when I get a dog, I'm going to teach it to say I love you" says the daughter defiantly.

fearing the answer, the mother is too afraid to ask why.

they stand up and leave the cafe together.

Josiah And His Hair

Josiah and his silent friend are walking with me
through the meadows
And he is telling me the story of his hair
This is hair worth a story
Part flat top, part dreadlocks
No medusa coils
If these dreadlocks were alive
They would be smiling, sunbathing, sleepy snakes.

Josiah says:
"When I was little, I had an afro
Combed it every day
Discovered that the big girls from big school liked to stroke
my hair
Discovered that I liked that too"

And Josiah says:
"Then I got a flat top
Urban flavour
Sharp
Hard edged"

And Josiah says:
"My grandmother
Buffalo soldier all her life
Wore her dreads wrapped in fabric from home
Flashes of red and yellow and green
My grandmother died"

And Josiah says:
"So, these locks remind me that my grandmother is always with me"

And when I look
I see his shoulders are broad enough to bear this burden.

I Cannot Write A Novel Today

I cannot write a novel today because...

1. My friend is writing poetry for gerbils and I need to watch the letter box for the manuscript, small and brown, a forgettable butterfly of verse.

2. The towels in my airing cupboard cry out to be arranged not just by size and colour, but fluffiness, fraying and the frisson of pleasure they give against warm damp skin.

3. Somewhere, out there, the perfect shoes exist - red, patent leather, kitten heeled, whimsical lacing and my feet are restless with longing.

4. The sofa groans with undiscovered hidden treasures, chocolate coins, half smoked cigarettes, a tiny china rabbit, I feel the urge for urban archaeology.

5. The dog seems depressed, not in touch with his inner wolf, I try to cheer him up by baying at the moon, it's the least I can do.

6. Somebody has updated their status, a photograph of mashed potatoes, onion gravy, steaming sausages, I need to comment - *yum yum*.

7. The horse needs me to stand, one foot resting on a gate, my chin against the sun warmed metal of the fastening, watching her eat grass.

8. The ducks are all in disarray, facing the wrong way on the bathroom shelf, if ignored, disaster will certainly follow.

9. The biscuit tin contains only cut-price own label digestives, nobody can expect creativity on such poor fare.

10. There are blue pens in the black pen jar and felt tips with the wrong colour lids and Duplo in the Lego box and the 'My Little Ponies' are missing their mane combs.

I cannot write a novel today.

Debt

And afterwards, saved from jumping, from falling,
he looks directly at her, *"I will always be in your debt"*
he says and she nods, appraising the truth of this
statement.

At first it is easy, a request to mend a dripping tap,
chop wood for her stove, drive her and a sickly pet
to the vets.

He is happy to help, after all he is in her debt.

But the tasks become more complex, long journeys
to collect objects she says she cannot live without,
heavy manual labour around her home, jobs that
take up more and more of his free time.

He considers refusing, but the pause she leaves
after each request reminds him that there is a debt
to be paid.

And then of course, there are the calls, late at night,
rambling into silence or diatribes about the
unfairness of her life.

He begins to dread the sound of his phone.

He makes his preparations, travels to the beach, weighs his pockets down with stones and walks towards the water.
He feels only relief, release.

He has made sure that she is out of town this weekend.

When Jamie Becomes Becki

When Jamie becomes Becki, he feels lighter,
Dancing becomes a joy not a chore,
Outfits chosen, unchosen, finally discarded
in the tiny back bedroom where nobody goes
except him, and of course her.

When Jamie becomes Becki, he still likes to
drink pints,
Likes how the amber light reflects onto her
sharp red nails,
Sometimes wishes that drinks are served in two
pint mugs.

Wishes that her hands could be dwarfed as they
wrap around the glass,
But shrugs, makes the best of things,
Her Pandora bracelet tapping against the rim
Chink, chink chink.

When Jamie becomes Becki, it is enough in itself,
enough for him, enough for her,
No endgame except the possibility
of near seduction in forgiving light,
The possibility of almost passing.

I Am Watching The Swans With
Shane MacGowan

I am standing with Shane, safe in the shadow of the
Martello Tower, built to warn the invaders, the
interlopers, that others might come, blown across
the grey sea, with their own plans to take this poor
land.

We are watching the swans, Children of Lir,
huddled in the harbour, buffeted against the jetty.
Their plumage, snow-white, bone-white against the
customary grey, brown of the Irish sea, interlopers
and alongside them, other outsiders. The yachts,
playthings of the playboys of the western world, or
at least the western coasts.

These yachts belong somewhere else, somewhere
with azure seas, skies that blend, fall from other
shades of blue into the gentle swell, not this
landscape of hard lines and cold breezes.

Shane discourses, poetry, womanizing, the arts of
falconry and warfare.
And we walk in the footsteps of poets and
warriors, taking the waters, but not the water of life
because Shane is drying out, drying up, moving
towards the years of silence.

I learnt to swim in the other harbour, concrete wall
built to trap the sea and in water so dark that we
could not see the bottom and so we learnt to swim,

a lesser terror than sinking into water we knew had
no ending, no sanctuary for feet, clenched in cold,
searching out safe harbour.

We never expected to find this sea swimming
pleasurable, water so cold it would
"knock the very breath out of ye"
and in homes where the threat to
"knock the very breath out of ye, see if I won't"
was commonplace, the sea held no fear for us.

The cold a rightful punishment for almost pleasure,
Catechism reinforced
"Who made the world?"
"God made the world"

I wonder what Shane looked at, that winter, when
the sea and sky met, bands of grey and brown and
white, dirty white, another shade of pale, a million
miles from the plumage of those swans rocked
against the winter waves.

I wonder if he looked out to sea or turned inward,
inland.

The Italian chipper, occasional destination,
wrapped in cardigans and anoraks, our knees and
lips blued from over immersion in the sea.
These chips, our reward for childhood bravery,
child stoicism, we ate them, huddled ourselves
against the constant winds, hot, greasy, somehow
more delicious the colder that we were.

And then, we walked past the Amusement arcade,
because nice children don't go there, licking the
tang of salt, sea salt, chip salt from our fingers as
the purple faded from our knees, our lips.

I am standing in the shelter of the Martello Tower,
taking refuge from a storm, one eye on the horizon,
grey and brown and white.

Watching for interlopers.

Best Road Trip Ever

The younger dog is puzzled
All this activity bears the hallmark of a day out
An adventure, a road trip
Leads collected
Dog bags discovered
Keys lost
Keys found
He positions himself at the front door
To ensure that he is first into the car

But,

Unaccountably, today he is left behind
Home alone
He stands at the window
Nose pressed against the glass
Confident that a mistake has been made
An error occurred
A wrong to be righted

Today is a one woman
One dog
One-way road trip

So,

You let her sit in the front seat
Open the window
In case she wants to stand on tippy paws
To hurl abuse at other dogs in other cars

But,

She is tired
Sighs, curls up like a kitten
Perks up when you open a bag of treats
Before you even reach the end of your street

You drive one-handed
Traffic Saturday morning light
This time chosen carefully
To avoid any danger of meets with colleagues later
Today as you know
That punching someone in the face will not play
Out well on some internal disciplinary sheet

You hand feed pieces of bite sized chicken
Cheese, salami, all the good stuff
And she sighs again, but this time with piggy greed

In the car park you sit, engine running
While you rub her belly and she, tailless
Wags her whole body in pleasure
While you eat the final sliver of cheese
Wish that you could freeze this moment forever
The waiting room is empty
First appointment of the day, candle already alight
So you wait, stroke velvet soft ears
Push back the inevitable tsunami of tears

Not now, not here

And afterwards
When the vet tells you that you can collect her on
Thursday
You look at his face, his lips
Can't understand what he's trying to say
Until it dawns on you, he means the box of dog
Dust and not her at all

At home, the younger dog is pleased to see you
Covers you in dog breath kisses
Invites you to a game of bark, nip, run
It is only hours later, after his careful examination
Of the garden, the dog beds and the rooms upstairs
That he finally stands at the front door
Stares at you
Confident that a mistake has been made
An error occurred
A wrong to be righted.

Be More Dog

Be more dog they say
so
I'm shedding language like fur
clawing only to words that give shape and meaning
to the day and I'm learning to tilt my head to one
side
When you speak expressing interest
although quite frankly I only get about half of what
you say

I won't judge by colour of skin or the cut of your
jib
But whether when we meet
you come down to my level
tell me I'm beautiful
offer something delicious to eat

Be more dog they say
so
I'll make as much noise as I want, and you can't
make me shush
and if I'm scared, I'll show it

Left alone for too long, I may make a mess of
things
and this may not be a figure of speech

Be more dog they say
so
I'll turn my belly to the sun
and my face to the sky
and fit 7 years of living into each 12 months
cos when you're a dog, time flies

Be more dog they say
so
I'll eat when I'm hungry
and eat when I'm full
walk straight past those mirrors
and if I'm with you, well, I'll just make you look
more cool

Be more dog.

Rescue Me

This is for Ryan and Niko (and the dogs of course)

The Polish dog is old
A little moth-eaten, shabby around her seams
She resembles nothing less than a much-loved
greying bear

My dogs are small, sometimes overawed by the
rumbustious play of bigger beasts
But
They enjoy her undemanding company
So
Sometimes we walk together
The Polish dog, the Polish boy and us

He says:
"She is shy"

He says:
"My stepfather used to beat her"
(and I see him choosing to not go there, not today)

He says:
*"But if you give her time and space, allowing her to set the
pace, she will stand near, and let you touch her"*

And when we stop, so that she can rest, she does
just that
Head just reaching his knees
Leaning in

Milky eyes fixed upon his face

My dogs are bored now, cast around for excitement
See Indi explode though the park gates
Indi, spent the first 6 months of her life in a room
Because no-one seemed to know that dogs need
walks, fresh air and other dogs

A different outfit every day
Plenty of Instagram likes, but not much love
Finally rescued and rehomed to the yoga teacher
Indi, making up for lost time
Everyday a birthday

We walk together and the boys lean into each other
with an easy intimacy, say something I don't quite
catch

And later the yoga teacher says
"We are together"

He says:
"We met here, on this park, because of the dogs"

He says:
"We are happy"

And it is a tiny everyday miracle
The dogs, the boys, the park
But blink, blink and you might miss it.

[3] Things That Have Happened / Will Happen / May Not Happen

Bovvered…Question Mark

1. *"My mums got a new boyfriend...proper wasteman...but I'm not bovvered".*

2. *"My stepdad threw my phone down the stairs, smashed the screen and everything...but I'm not bovvered".*

3. *"He said the photos were just for us, everyone at school's seen them now...but I'm not bovvered".*

4. *"My uncle's a right pedo..."* and for a moment, the mask almost slips, but then it's jammed back into place with a ferocious anger, *"but he's not fucking touching me and anyway...I'm not bovvered".*

And, in the room with no windows at the end of the corridor, today, we are not bothered about Shakespeare or Steinbeck.

We are especially not bothered about the committing to memory of 16 or 17 random poems, just to prove we could all have had a grammar school education.

And, I'm trying really hard to not be bothered by the simple fact that half this class can't read well enough to even understand the questions on a G.C.S.E examination paper.

Shamima, 15 years old and a virgin on your
wedding night was your warrior husband gentle,
playful even ?

Or, already battle shattered, did he grab at you with
hot, hard hands while you lay still, face blank, not
bothered ?

And, later, did you run your hands over the thick
black fabric that enveloped you, shrouded your
swelling belly ?

Or, were you already fatalistic, a shrug, Insha'Allah,
if he wills it and later still, when you held your first
and your second and your third dead baby, were
you bothered then ?

Or, did you seek refuge in the rhetoric of
revolution ?

Shamima, you would never have ended up in the
windowless room at the end of the corridor
you were, by all accounts, bright, hardworking, able
but, in some other classroom, with light and air and
a whiteboard that actually bloody works, were you
already learning to keep your head down, face
blank, still, not bothered while you waited for
something to happen ?

And back in that windowless room at the end of that long corridor...

Siddik, and M² and Leyton and Tenika and Tequila and Saffron and Joey and Ami with an 'i'

are still not bothered,

are still,

are waiting for the next thing to happen.

Scream

I screamed
you didn't hear me.

Higher Patrick, higher, push me higher than I've
ever been.

The seagulls screamed in the sky above
where our eyes meet.

Scream me a love song, kiss me before I scream
skrik, scream, shriek.

I am screaming with a deflated lung
silently, desperately trying to reach.

My father, screaming, rattling the walls
screaming underwater.

Scream, scream, scream, hard to catch his breath
screaming with deflated lungs.

Infinite screams
slaughterhouse and asylum.

Skrik, Scream, Shriek.

Screaming in silence to ears turned deaf
I have no mouth, but I must scream.

Sat Nav

I need a sat nav for my life
I want updates on congestion in the corridors
And more crucially, congestion in my chest.

I need a sat nav for my life
But not the shouty ones
The ones that scream turn left
When you have already missed the junction.

Instead a honey tongued siren who will whisper
"Turn around when you are able"
An understand it may take time
Before I find a turn that I can take.

I need a sat nav for my life
I want to know when I'm on uneven ground
On thin ice
Heading to deep water.

On days when I can't dress
I need a sat nav to give advice
"At the 3rd hanger take the first item"
(in fairness, many of my clothes are double parked).

I need a sat nav for my life
"Re-configuring your journey"
When everything seems lost
And a sat nav that will re-boot
To take the scenic route

To remind me that fast and straight
Are not the only ways
To reach your destination.

I need a sat nav for my life
Even when it says we're here
And here just looks like everywhere
And so, I keep on driving
And maybe that's the point.

I need a sat nav for my life.

Firewatching

My grandfather cycles at a careful deliberate pace
too fast and the dynamo will make the bike lights
burn too bright, too slow and they will flicker,
falter, fail, no light matter in war darkened Dublin

My grandfather is going firewatching
all night he will stand, binoculars in hand, surveying
the sky

His war quality woollen muffler chafes the back of
his neck, this scarf has been knitted, badly, by the
family's itinerant maid

This same woman, who each day will swaddle my
mother in her shawl, a shawl that smells of cheap
tobacco, porter, peat, a smell my mother still
remembers almost 90 years on

At the end of his uneventful shift my grandfather
will cycle home but this time faster, as light creeps
over the Wicklow hills, with a final delicious
freewheel down Roebuck Rd and then a sharp left
into his own drive

In daytime, there are drills, alarms sounded, all
clears given, Dubliners, least herdable people in the
world look up, they all have cousins in London,
Birmingham, Coventry, know what the skies can
bring

But, secure in their neutrality, they shrug, agree that
Hitler is a terrible auld eejit, go back to daily living

My grandmother sniffs
sees these drills as showing off
goes off about her daily business
queues for jam where raspberry pips have been
replaced with chips of wood and where no-one
recognises the names of fish at the fishmonger

He swears they taste like plaice
they never do

My grandfather missed the one night of air-based
action,
a German bomber
off path
off plan
misjudged their route
tried to jettison the contents of their bomb bays
into Dublin Bay,
misjudged again
took out a row of terraced houses

Decades later, I lie at his feet,
unravelling knots in a Persian rug,
I clutch my newest Enid Blyton to my chest
clutch, but don't read because I'm trying to make it
last
even babies of war babies know the importance of
rationing pleasure

My grandfather's regret at missing his one chance
for heroism is palpable even to me
My grandmother, heard it all before, sniffs and in
the absence of any help these days, goes off to
make a pot of tea

I know I shouldn't, really shouldn't, but like any
addict, convince myself that this time it will be
alright and if it isn't then I can easily retune to
Classic FM, Smooth radio, lose myself in dance hits
of the 90s

But instead, I am listening to radio 4
insect extinction
antibiotic resistance
and a clear-eyed child telling me that I should panic
about climate change, panic as if my own house
were on fire

And I wish I had my grandfathers' binoculars
wish I felt their heavy weight of certainty
wished like him I believed that this is a world worth
fighting for

Their faces say that we know that we are part of
history
and they are watching Notre Dame burn
half a world away, smaller less important churches
are burning too
A different sort of priceless artifact inside

Children dressed in Easter Sunday best
dresses with sticky out skirts
gleaming patent shoes

Some carrying small baskets of painted eggs

It's best, I find, to not think about those painted
eggs

In this war there are no drills, no all clear sounded
sometimes, like those people back by Dublin Bay
it's just poor luck
wrong time, wrong place

And I wish we all had my grandfather's binoculars
all felt their heavy weight of certainty
all believed with him that this is a world worth
fighting for

We are all firewatchers now.

Cracked...

You thought this cup would last forever
Victorian bone china so fine the rim had a ring like
a bell
And you were careful
Used it sparingly
Enveloped it in tissue paper
Bubble wrap
But not enough
You failed to see the flaw that threatened form
Until one day it cracked
Left you holding two perfectly imperfect halves
And you dropped
Part shock
Part moderate scald
But it's hard to keep your footing when you're
already on thin ice
And it's not the shiny stuff you need to fear
The stuff that says be careful
Slipping hazard here
It's the other stuff
The sneaky stuff that takes you unaware
That makes you less than biped
And even when you clamber up
You're not the same
You've suffered some sea change
But it's hard to keep your footing when you're
already on thin ice
And not everything has a warning light
Even things that should
And anyway, they're easy to ignore

To keep on driving
Put those letters in a drawer
Convince yourself on sleepless nights that
somehow everything will be alright
But it's hard to keep your footing when you're
already on thin ice
And every time you fall
You come back somehow less
Tissue of scars on tissue paper skin so thin that
every jolt will make you bleed
And muscle memory pain reminds you that you
will
You will
You will
Fall down again
And it's easy to lose your footing when you're
already on thin ice

[4] Love *Slash* Not Love

A Poem On The Importance Of Careful Measurement Prior To Committing To Ownership

We went to Brighton to buy a bed
New couple yes, but hardly loves young dream
But

Sill in need to extra space for languid lounging,
endless pots of tea
Love will find a way we said

So, failed to measure car or bed
And failed again
Forced to leave it there beside the sea

And even if we'd brought it back
Nowadays it would be full of me and a pack of
snoring dogs

But

Sometimes I do wonder that if we'd found that
special way
Whether we'd still be together
If only for the sake of the furniture

Hashtag 'Me Too'

He said he liked my sweatshirt, said Wonder
Woman was his favourite when he was a kid
hashtag me too
I see your compliment and raise you

This boy in my French class keeps staring at me
hashtag me too
I see your gaze and raise you

They made us read a book where a woman got hurt
in olden times
hashtag me too
I see your triggering literature and raise you

When he reached across my desk to get a paper
clip, his hands brushed my shoulder
hashtag me too
I see your uninvited touch and raise you

In the pub, with work friends, he made a joke
about big breasted women
hashtag me too
I see your banter and raise you

He asked my friend to ask me if I fancied a drink
sometime
hashtag me too
I see your assumptive behaviour and raise you

When we kissed, he put his tongue inside my
mouth
hashtag me too
I see your boundary pushing and raise you

We got drunk, we had bad sex, in the morning, I
wish we hadn't
hashtag me too
I see your issues around consent and raise you

He told me that I had to choose, him or my friends
hashtag me too
I see his controlling behaviour and raise you

He told me it would really help my grades if I had
one-to-one tutorials with him on a Sunday morning
at his house
hashtag me too
I see his abuse of power and raise you

He pushed me into a doorway and told me he had
a knife
hashtag me too
I see your stranger rape and raise you

My father only touched me when he was very
drunk
hashtag me too
I see the child abuse and raise you

This Is Not A Love Song

But
You make art and music and good bread
And never forget that I don't like butter,
So, on picnics, my sandwiches are sliced separately,
wrapped differently, ensuring that only I get to
enjoy their delicious dryness,

                                    And this is not a love song

But
As a DJ, you kept your head down,
Mujahideen hat just visible above the decks,
Not really a *'Hands In The Air Like You Just Don't
Care'* kind of guy,

But,
Just occasionally, if it was going well,
you would risk a smile and then a quick   1   2
1   2   3
soft shoe shuffle,

                                    And this is not a love song

But,
When my daughter was tiny new,
You held her, fitting perfectly into your cupped
palms,
Not a father, never a father,
Bound to her with ties other than blood,
Maybe better,

                                    And this is not a love song,

But
You have learnt to slow down, to keep pace with
your father,
Learnt to bite back irritation when you have the
same conversation
for the 3rd or 4th time today,
Learnt to cook meals where the meat and
vegetables
are clearly delineated on the plate,

And this is not a love song

But
Over the years you have
Supported my attempts at dressage mediocrity
Scouted backgrounds for photo shoots to meet my
social media neediness
And always, always, always preview horror films to
check that I can take them.

And this is not a love song,

But,

This is not a love song.

The Saddest Thing

This thing.

This thing is the saddest thing.

This is sadder than the face my dog pulls when a bigger dog steals her tennis ball and runs away with it.

This is sadder than the time someone told me I was a poor friend and my first thought was, well no more late-night drama laden phone calls from you then.

Sadder than my mother's fridge, a neat line of pale blue saucers, each containing a tablespoon of left-over lunch and in the fridge door, 5 unopened cartons of milk, just in case.

This is sadder than when at 17, 18, 19, your heart broken for the first time, you lay on the bed, quite convinced that you would die, because who could endure such pain.

Sadder even, then when later, at 40, 50, 60, veteran of multiple failures of heart, you know all too well that you will survive this break and the next and the next.

This is sadder than food banks
Sadder than my neighbour, beginning to lose
language, beginning to feel meaning slip away.

This is sadder than the boy in the doorway, his dog
wrapped in a coat and a duvet, snug as a bug in a
rug, but when I look down, he is wearing shoes,
but no socks.

This is the very saddest thing

This is the hearse, and this is the coffin that doesn't
fill it. And all the flowers and helium balloons and
teddies in the world cannot erase this space, cannot
fill this gap, cannot hide this hole.

This is the very, very saddest thing

And then the lights change, and they turn left, and
I execute a clumsy right-hand manoeuvre.
It's hard to drive well when you're crying for
someone else's saddest thing.

Valentine's Day

its Valentine's Day
and the traffic is at a standstill
gridlocked
we're going nowhere
and I'm tapping

no, actually I'm punching the steering wheel
"come on, come on, come on"
as if my voice alone can make movement.

its Valentine's Day
and all over my network
Bunny Bookins is wishing Mr Fluffy a really special
day
And Kevin is wondering if you want to play hide
the carrot…later

my texts are terser
I'm on my way, I'm coming, please wait, just wait.

its Valentine's Day and every song on the radio
is a fucking love song
and now I'm starting to sob
those shoulder shaking, snot making sobs.

and I'm seriously considering just driving down the
hard shoulder
I'm sorry officer, it was an emergency and besides
its Valentine's Day.

the man in the stationary van next to me has had
enough time now
to see that something's not right
so, he gets out, taps on the window, asks if I'm ok

and I look at him
hair standing on end
snail trail tracks of tears
mascara on my chin
I nod and smile and tell him I'm fine.

its Valentine's Day and finally, we're moving,
a miracle
and I make a 40-minute journey in 25
and when I get there,
you're still there,
you're still there
and you make that special noise of recognition
that
bpppphhhhhhhh

so, we feed you mints and carrots and apples
all your favourite things
and afterwards, the vet hands me your headcollar
and lead rope.

and it's Valentine's Day
and I'm driving home alone
my thumb brushing over the brass buckle of your
best headcollar
your leather high days and holidays headcollar
and I'm beginning to understand that this
this is going to be my Valentine's Day memory.

Room

1. *Yellow*

We painted the walls sunshine yellow
A busy frieze of buses, bikes and boats because we
weren't going to buy into any gender stereotypes

Hung mobiles, placed posters
Carefully fitted cherry red handles to door and
drawers, ensuring we left no sharp edges.

2. *Pink*

Already feeling the space between you, other
children and the world
I chose the pinkest pink I could find
Festooned every surface with fairy lights
A cabin bed with a tower of teddies standing
sentinel

Stack boxes each with a picture of what lived inside
for ease of tidying
And on your special shelf, your treasures, silver
fairy wings, a horseshoe from your first pony and
one bear, too precious to be part of the cuddle toy
hoi polloi.

3. *Accent wall*

The accent wall is black and white abstracted
flowers
So, black desk, black duvet on the bed that made
into a sofa
Your pad I called it
You hung posters of bands whose names I didn't
know
And I learnt to knock
Learnt that often your choice was not to let me in.

4. *White*

The walls are utilitarian white now
Filthy with handprints, footprints, smeared
makeup, other stains
Your bed a mattress on the floor, after you
destroyed the third bed in some inarticulate howl
of rage
I stopped replacing them, stopped repairing
furniture, stopped worrying about the shards of
shattered mirror glass

I used to make speedy sorties inside when I had
run out of plates, bowls and cups
Excavating only the top layer

Careful not to see the unfilled prescriptions, the
unattended appointments

Now I just buy new crockery.

5. *Doors and walls*

I'm waiting for the day when the police want to
look inside this room, will want to look for clues,
will want to look for meaning

We will stand on the threshold, me squirming with
shame, they already on task
I will smile some terrible social smile
Tell them how sorry I am, tell them how nice it
used to be in here.

5 Minutes

If she waits 5 minutes longer, he may least have got his pants on.

If she waits 5 minutes longer, the other woman in their bed may have taken the dressing gown off.

If she waits 5 minutes longer, she may not have to hear the grunting, animal noises as she drops her car keys into the fruit bowl on the kitchen table.

If she waits 5 minutes longer, they may have uncoupled and be able to at least look her in the eye.

If she waits 5 minutes longer, she may not need to follow the trail of clothes up the cord carpeted stairs.

If she waits 5 minutes longer, she may miss the exit of the neat black sports car from her gravelled drive.

If she waits 5 minutes longer, she may meet, head on, that car losing control on the tight bend just before she turns for home.

Crossing The Line

Straddled
face squashed into a pillow
focusing on his breathing
in and out and in and out
don't show the fear.

Tonight, he knows that a line will be crossed
that after tonight, there will be no going back.
She has said as much
prepared him carefully.

Ice
and fire
and chains
and now this line to cross.

He feels her weight shift against his shoulder blades
one hand against the top of his spine
fingers pressing on individual vertebrae
pressure just the other side of pleasure
her breath on the nape of his neck as she leans
towards him
her hands swooping down towards the small of his
back.

He stiffens
bites back a sound, almost a moan
stays still
stays silent
And then there is a pause
a waiting.

His skin electric with anticipation
twitches
The first cut comes so fast that he has no time to
process what has happened
is only aware of sound
not pain
just the click of the unsheathed blade
the sush of skin scored like silk
And then, two more
zip
zip.

And afterwards
she takes him to a mirror
gently
tenderly
her fingers on his neck
tilting his head so that he can see
3 neat lines
Line 1
Line 2
Spine
Line 3
He knows that he crossed another line.

That Was Then And This Is Now

At 18 I was careless,
Let things slip through my fingers, pretty boys,
opportunities, a fabulous Biba frock,
confident that around the corner was a bigger,
better, shiny thing.

At 58, things still slip through my fingers, arthritis
clawing at my joints,
I'm losing my grip
And around this corner is probably another corner.

At 18, in the room, in the squatted house, on the
street that nestled beneath the 3 tower blocks,
I filled the space with mirrors, papered the walls
with pages torn from the glossy magazines that Jem
stole so stylishly from the better department stores.

On days where there was not much going on, we
recreated those photos, expressed dissatisfaction,
but each of us secretly a little in love with our own
reflection.

At 58, there are days when I don't recognise the
woman who smiles hesitantly at me from plate-
glass windows.

At 18 I was all about brazen presence,
Walking through the market at 6am
Grey fedora hat
Men's vest slashed just below my breasts

No bra and on my feet workmen's boots, spray painted silver.

At 58 in my sensible dog walking coat and my sensible dog walking shoes and my sensible dog walking hat, I am almost not here.

The boys who congregate on the park to smoke weed are solicitous when they spill from their bench onto the path *"mind"* says one, *"that lady needs to get by"*

At 18 I knew everything I would ever need to know
At 58, I tentatively offer these 3 truths
Dogs are better than hot water bottles
You cannot own enough pairs of reading glasses
And never take a good night's sleep for granted.

Fabulous Styling Tips For Fashion Forward Funerals

Black....well duh.
The 'go-to' choice,
respectful and respectable.

A million Victorian matrons can't be wrong.
See them swathed in serge and velvet and
bombazine.
A year of black and then grief dependant,
move to purple or grey or sensible navy blue.

Black
is the colour of my true love's hair.
Black
is the colour of suburban goth,
the colour of the beatnik,
the colour of the broken-hearted.

But, black drains you,
everyone knows that and today,
if she is drained of anything else,
she will be weightless,
nothing left, an empty husk
and may simply float away,
carried by the winds,
drifting
above this car
on this journey.

White,
think of all those tiny wizened Asian widows
wrapped in layers of silk and cotton
something fragile to be protected
White widows,
sometimes with an incongruous pop of colour,
a fire engine red Pac A Mac, lime green crocs, a
tartan shopping trolley on wheels.

And white is the colour of virgins,
of bridal nights and lost innocence
and in this, her new state, she too is virginal,
touched for the very last time.
And although her anger is white-hot,
burning hot, her grief is making her clumsy,
awkward.
White requires too much poise, a neatness and a
lack of tears.

Red,
red for passion and roses and Valentine's Day
and god knows there was passion and hearts
and flowers and unsuitable underwear in not quite
the right size.

And red says, warning and danger
and look at me
and red says stop.

Stop, she thinks,
I want this to stop,
but all the traffic lights in the world
cannot stop this journey, in this car, to that place.

All week, the women in her phone
have been sending soft fabric packages,
some have come with long letters,
Some just signed with a kiss,
but all have added those five letters,
Their rallying call when life gives you fucking
lemons, again.

CCUYB
(chin chin, up your bum)

Don't be a lady
Don't dress for your age
Don't be quiet
Most of all, don't be quiet
Do not go quietly into this or any other dark night.

The women in her phone have been sending her
things
A sequined jacket
A leopard print beret
A dress of spots and stripes and stars
But most of all, they have been sending her
lipsticks,
red lipsticks,

some clearly expensive,
nestling in black velvet drawstring bags,
others picked up in the weekly grocery shop,
dropped into the trolley, their purchase easy to hide
from cock wombles and non cock wombles alike.

Lip sticks have names and right now,
in this car on this journey
she finds herself head bowed,
lips moving, not in prayer,

There is no prayer to make this better,
but instead she lists all the names of all the lipsticks
now littering her dressing table.

Obsessed
999
Ruby Woo
Dragon Girl
Devil
Pirate
Fire and Ice
Underage Kiss

She is surprised how comforting this is.

[5] The Chi Chi Trilogy

More And More I Find Myself Thinking About Chi Chi The Panda (1)

It is the 1970s and the TV is black and white, there are colour TVs of course, but they still have a black and white one and sometimes that's a problem.

Sometimes when other children come around, they notice, notice the TV, notice the holes in the carpet in the hallway, notice the saucepan instead of a kettle.
But pandas work well in black and white.

It is the first time that she can remember actually watching the grown-up news, properly watching, not just waiting for it to finish and she sees the panda being carried down the steps of an aeroplane.

Weeks pass and the panda story grows,
Chi Chi the panda has come all the way from China, she is a present from China.

But not a present you get yourself

She is a present for everyone

Whenever she is on TV, there are always men in suits and the kind of hats dads wear when they go to work.
A famous architect has designed her new home at London Zoo.

London Zoo is in London which is a long way
away from where they live.

For Christmas, the child asks for a panda, really she
wants Chi Chi or at least the chance to go all the
way to London to see the real Chi Chi, but she
does get a small fluffy black and white bear, she
calls it Chi Chi
Plans to make a zoo home for her out of a
cardboard box on the day after Boxing day when
they have nothing special to do.

She also receives;
A famous five book
A selection box
A wade whimsy china rabbit
A new swimming costume
A charm for her charm bracelet, she has nine now
and wears the bracelet all day on Christmas Day.

On Christmas Day evening, when the adults are
opening a bottle of wine
and all the nice quality street have been eaten,
she lies quietly on her bed
and strokes the bear's soft fur
and whispers her name out loud
Chi Chi
Chi Chi
Chi Chi.

More And More I Find Myself Thinking About Chi Chi The Panda (2)

The woman is being driven through London in a
Triumph Spitfire in a heat wave
It is sometime in the 90s

The car is not hers.
The man is not her husband.
Even the year does not feel like her year

But the child, shoehorned into a space
not really big enough for anything larger than an
overnight bag,
the child is most definitely hers.

And the child is the reason for this trip,
this jaunt, the Sunday afternoon educational outing.

They are driving through London in a sports car to
the Natural History Museum
to look at dinosaurs and polar bears, to press
buttons and read tiny labels.
They are going to have fun.

The husband, the car, the A to Z and a possibly
misjudged Vivienne Westwood frock are all on
loan, borrowed from a friend who childless herself
does not quite see that a museum in August
may not be fun.
They may not have fun.

The man has never been to a museum with a child,
he is not prepared for the whirlwind of movement,
the restless gallop from thing to thing,
the urgency of what's next.

What's next?

The child sees the gift shop,
latches onto a leopard head hat, furry, fully lined,
designed for winter days.
It is a ridiculous item on a day when the sun
has made the seats so hot
that the mother has spent the whole drive
lifting her thighs away from heat,
hoping that this wriggling will be read for what it is
by the borrowed husband
in this borrowed car.

The tearoom is in the basement,
Cool, green tiled, surprisingly deserted
and there, by the entrance is a panda,
a stuffed panda in a glass display case.

Even the child stops for a moment
and then walks up to the case and looks carefully at
what's inside.
A slightly discoloured stuffed animal,
A wall of black and white photos
and a small pyramid of
less discoloured soft toys.
The woman joins her and then realises

that this is not just *a* panda, this is Chi Chi *the*
panda.
This is the panda from her childhood,
her first memory of watching the grown-up news.
The man,
the not husband, is standing next to her, he shakes
his head
"*Sad*" he says "*Poor animal, on her own for so many
years.*"
He and the child head towards the counter,
queuing, looking at cake,
both eyeing up the very pink ones with many, many
smarties on top.

Heat hits hard as they hit the pavement
child impervious insists on wearing the leopard
headed hat,

They drive away, to return the husband, the car, the
A to Z and the frock
to their rightful owner.

The only evidence of the woman's silent tears
are tiny water damage spots on the silk on the left
sleeve of the borrowed dress.

Chi Chi…Going Home

The best thing that ever happened to me.

I don't go out much anymore, the light hurts my
eyes, my old bones ache
I am tired of the whoops, the shouts each time I
appear
I stay inside. That fact is well known
a sign outside my enclosure warns the public
against disappointment.

There is nothing to see here, not for you, not for
me. I have lived in this concrete approximation of
my home for 14 years
really there is nothing to see here, move on, move
on.

It is summer, or what they call summer, sticky, hot,
the smell of fatty food in the air
these are the only summers I remember clearly, but
when I sit in the dark, my back against the wall, I
can remember another time
a time of cool green, of the taste of fresh bamboo a
vivid moment of crunch in my mouth.

The memory teases me, not quite caught, not ready
to be pinned down, examined, understood.

It's gone quiet now
the constant drone of voices is over, all I can hear
is the murmur of far away traffic and of course my
own heart, not beating as strongly as it used to
a little hesitant now
a tiny pause between each beat, each breath.

The man stays, my breath ragged now, each
heartbeat an effort, the pauses longer between each
gasp
the jungle thread begins to pull me back. I feel the
dappled sunlight against my fur.

I am going home.

[6] To Do And Not To Do

I Remember Everyone I Have Ever Slept With

1. I remember everyone I have ever slept with, even though I may have forgotten many of their names.

2. I remember the first time and afterwards, a shame faced entry into a sitting room where everyone knew our business.

3. I remember the last time with R, with nothing left to say, we took refuge under the duvet on a wet September day.

4. I remember sharing a bed with B, she carefully placed pillows down the centre line, a demarcation of distance, of decency and decorum.

5. I remember the man who would knock on my door at midnight and fool that I was, I would always let him in.

6. I remember spooning against A, his aubergine skin against mine, so dark it made my Irish whiteness glow in the soft light of my bedroom.

7. I remember summer afternoons with J, lolling on a grubby mattress on the floor, we stuck our feet out of the window to cool ourselves and waved them at passers-by.

8. I remember another J, in a tent where we pressed our hands against each other's mouths so that we would not wake the other campers.

9. I remember, drunk on cava and sun, sharing a bed with my mother, we talked and giggled until the children, over-tired and fractious, told us to shut up and go to sleep.

10. I remember the stone-cold dyke, sprawled across my pillows, fully dressed as she watched me through half closed, calculating eyes.

11. I remember sleeping with A in a tipi and waking to find snowflakes drifting across our sleeping bag.

12. I remember a caravan in Norfolk and a small child pretending to be asleep while waiting for Christmas morning.

13. I remember dozing with the un-named Greenham women while we waited for morning and yet another eviction.

14. I remember Ns' bed, so dipped and broken that we rolled together into an inevitable embrace, blaming fate & bad carpentry.

15. I remember sleeping with an almost famous comedian who insisted on leaning his double base case at the foot of my bed. It loomed over us all night.

16. I remember New Year's Eve 1999, D threw pillows at my head when I talked in my sleep.

17. I remember Ms' home-made bed - 6 feet off the floor, we slept like over-sized birds in a wooden nest.

18. I remember an unnamed man who woke me to tell me that my cats were staring at him.

19. I remember sharing a bed with my sister, we slept top to tail, whispering and watching the flames die down in the bedroom grate.

20. I remember another R, we would listen to the shipping forecast late at night and he, claiming to be a sailor, would tell me tales of the sea, in retrospect, I see that many of these stories were fictions.

21. I remember M who in my freezing flat, wore his badly darned yellow jumper as some defence against the cold.

22. I remember a cat, who while I slept, gave birth to 3 tabby kittens.

23. I remember A who swore me to secrecy.

24. I remember the night I lured a model home and the look of disbelief on the faces of those left in the club who watched us leave.

25. I remember the husky dog, as the night went on, she would move herself further and further up the bed, until, finally, her head would rest on a pillow, face staring into mine.

26. I remember small bear, wearer of tiny knitted trousers to stop his sawdust innards leaking.

27. I remember staggering home from a dentist, mouth full of blood and H who lay on top of the blanket, patting my hand until the pain killers kicked in.

28. All, many, some of these may be true, un-true, mis-remembered.

Feral Boys That I Have Fucked

Take 1

His inexpert scrabbling in your bag wakes you and when he realises that you are watching him through half closed eyes, face propped up into an approximation of alertness, he ducks his head, smiles and shrugs.
Stepping away from the bed, he locates his boots and retreats backwards towards the door, clutching them to his chest.

Take 2

He hid a gun in your microwave and although you liked the feeling of living at the edge, the inconvenience of not being able to heat tomato soup or zap potatoes got to you and finally, employing a logic that only occurs when you and everyone you know is doing a lot of cocaine, you wrapped the gun in layer upon layer of kitchen roll and dropped the package behind the washing machine.

Take 3

In the days before text messaging and booty calls, at 3, 4 am, he would scratch and scrape at your door, like the oversized tom cat that he was. Stomping downstairs, body stiff with resentment and cold, it always seemed to be winter then, face still soft from sleep, you would vow to send him away this time.

And each time, his under-dressed body, shoulder blades sharp as vestigial wings, each rib delineated under an off black t-shirt beguiled you and you opened the door, wondering if there was enough milk for tea.

Take 4

You face each-other on the pillow, his mascara is smudged, eye liner slipped towards his cheek bones, there is a pause while you both take stock of where the evening has taken you.

You close your eyes, feign sleep, hope that when you open them again, he will be gone and then wonder where exactly you are and if instead it should be you who is going somewhere.

When you open them again, he is still there, quietly looking at you, you smile, hoping your face is less ruined than his and he smiles back.

Take 5

He enjoys taking you to clubs where he knows everyone and sometimes you dance together, but more usually, you dance and he watches, while people approach him and move away 2, 3 minutes later, nodding, smiling.

You pretend not to notice.

Sometimes he vanishes for hours and suddenly -re-appears, puffed up with self-importance.

You pretend not to notice.

And there are the women, always in the back of the car, never the front, that is where you sit.
He converses with them in angry whispers and no-one looks at you.

You pretend not to notice.

A Naming Of Parts

Your feet, bare, brown, gritty with memory of sand and salt, driving home sans shoes after a seaside day.

At night, my breath on the nape of your neck, most vulnerable of all skin, the neck inviting confidences.

The scar on your belly, my tongue traces the ghosts of stitching. Bites just enough to make you wince.

Wrists too large for me to circle with my fingers, curiously hairless, the skin there softer than your hand.

The dent in your nose, bone broken from a life before I knew you.

Your balls, strange fruit, cool to my touch, fitting exactly in a palm. Their weight a known certainty.

Shoulder blades like bird wings, sharp against my breasts when I lie behind you.

The curve of your spine, arching towards me as I play out each vertebrae in turn.

Your nipples stiffening with just my out breath as I whisper your name into your chest.

The smell of you, of musk and sweat and sex and cheap cigarettes and expensive cologne.

I name your parts, a mapping, a memory of senses, to keep you real, to keep you here.

Strategies To Survive A Summer Storm

Make no mistake, this is a snow day, sans snow. A day when all bets are off, routines abandoned, rhyme and rhythm lost.

This is not a day for useful enterprise, cupboard mining, tax returning or self-improvement.

Before it breaks, before the sturm and drang, stand and wait, wait at the window, on a balcony, in a garden. Wait in air so leaden with promise, with threat.

Dragged down, earthbound, in bondage.

Wait.

Light a cigarette and watch the smoke hang heavy, familiar tobacco scent cutting across a hint of metal, electricity in the air.

The first flash, first fork is a signal.

Gather together small children, pets and adults of a nervous disposition on a life raft of duvets on the largest double bed.

It is permissible to collect extra pillows, soft toys and snacks of a comforting nature to ensure survival on this journey.

Priority places should be allocated to those who can remember the techniques for calculating the exact distance of the storm from your roof top. This calculation can contribute to the primary numeracy curriculum and therefore this storm day is technically a learning day.

Relax.

No food or drink consumed on a storm day has any calories, fat or sugar content, but choose carefully, ensure that all snacks celebrate the spirit of summer storm.

Consider rum, hard bread, small fish.
If all else fails, choose crisps, conveniently packaged in water-proof bags.

Tell stories of storms gone past, remember to embellish.

The horse hit by lightning, its' metal shoes quadraphonic conductors.
The man drowned when the stream became a river, became a torrent, became the sea.
Mr Noah
Mrs Wolfe.

Be kind to those who become fearful, they are right, the gods are angry.
Do not share the statistics of the likelihood of lightning strike.

It will not help.

Exile, exile immediately, anyone who, peering into
the sky, suggests that
"It seems to be clearing up"

This is a day to catastrophise,
To watch the world wash away.
Street by street.

Eventually, you will have to succumb to the
irresistible rhythm of the rain on the roof.
Open the door, deep breath,
give yourself up to the storm.

A shower of power.

Stand and wave a fist at Thor and all the gods
whose names you have forgotten.

Or

If you are less heroic, more self-conscious,
sing quietly to yourself
*"I'm singing in the rain, just singing in the rain, what a
glorious feeling"*

and
as the
words peter out,
find a puddle to stamp in.

Things You Find At Bus Stops

1. A fox, eyes glittering, reflecting back in the headlights of the few cars that pass at 3am. He sits upright, primly at the front of a non-existent queue, for all the world as if he is waiting to catch the next bus to somewhere more interesting than this street of shuttered shops and dark terraced houses.

2. A dog lead and collar, red leather, small studs on the collar. The lead is looped neatly around the timetable post, secure, safe, no possibility of the dog slipping free, running blindly into the traffic, tied with care, with love. The absence of dog feels somehow more real in the half light of almost dawn.

3. A pair of 'fuck me' shoes, red, patent leather, impossible heels. Owner, feet on fire, insteps throbbing, a plaster dug out from the deepest recesses of a tiny bag, failing to cover the blistered heel, falling into the bus stop and in a moment of loathing, slipping the shoes off.

4. A thermos flask and a Tupperware container, containing one triangle of ham sandwich. The sandwich is neat, cut with a sharp knife, white sliced bread, ham, butter, a man's sandwich. The thermos flask is

elderly with a green checked pattern, fading into autumnal yellow.

5. A book, paperback, well used, pages turned down, spine starting to break. "Men are from Mars, Women are from Venus".

6. One pearl earring, delicate, expensive, the pearl set in gold. It is shining in the streetlights. In the morning, pecked by disappointed pigeons and pushed by busy work time feet, it will have rolled into the gutter and be lost among fast food wrapper and autumn leaves.

7. A mobile phone, fallen from a pocket and now under a seat. Later it will ring, but there will be no-one here to hear it.

8. A woman, hair and most of her face hidden, covered by niqab. Her heavy eye make-up is running, a trail of glittery green which vanishes into the heavy fabric. A tear falls from her eyes, her veil is sodden from crying.

9. A pair of false teeth.

10. A drunk man, half asleep and at his feet, wide awake, a chicken.

11. Two girls sit back to back on the red plastic chairs at the night bus stop. They lean into each other, sharing body heat. One is half asleep, eyes almost closed. She is humming the last track they heard at the club, still lost in music and the smell of sweat and fading perfume on her partners skin.

12. The pantomime horse, drooping now, weighed down by the heat of fake fur and tired of trying to talk through the mesh of the horse heads. The front hopes that the north bound bus will come first and that he can convince the back end to come back to his place.

The Woman Lists What Has Been Lost

Left Hand

1. A husband lost on a winters' day when
   waking she looked and saw a strangers' face
   on the pillow next to hers. The losing took
   more planning, more time, more effort than
   seemed possible once the decision had been
   made.

2. A grey velveteen rabbit, sewn by her
   grandmother, its button eyes, slightly
   uneven, giving it a constantly surprised
   expression. Left on a number 82 bus and
   never handed in, despite her insistence that
   her mother called at the lost property office
   week after week. It was years before she
   gave up hope of its return.

3. A diamond ring, borrowed without
   permission from the other grandmother,
   worn to impress a man who might have
   become her husband, but didn't. Her
   grandmothers' dementia saved her from the
   shame of ever admitting this theft.

4. A lipstick, pillar box red, the one worn
   when she feared invisibility, a statement
   color. A lipstick more exciting than she felt
   she could ever be. Its loss was somewhat of

a relief, allowing her to embrace pale rose, a more fitting shade.

5. A cat, black and white, 5 years old. For years afterwards, she would carefully examine any similarly colored animal until one day she realised that the cat, her cat would long be dead.

Right Hand

1. A friend, a friendship that lasted through school and college and small children and no sleep and no money but slipped away, quietly, almost unnoticed when there was nothing left to complain about anymore.

2. A car, but only briefly, in those days when life seemed to consist of lists and tasks and don't forgets. Parked on a day when her head felt so full that there was space for nothing else. A patient attendant walked from floor to floor with her until the car was found.
    No longer lost.

3. A t-shirt, out-sized, fabric softened by years of washing to become the perfect sleeping garment. Lost, madly, mysteriously within her own home. Some days, she opens a drawer, digs into a cupboard, and is

momentarily convinced that today will be the day when as mysteriously as it vanished, it will return.

4. A key, not her own, a key to someone else's house. She kept it, hanging uselessly on her own key ring, even though she never planned to open that door again .

5. A school duffle coat, bottle green, bought to grow into and finally, after several foiled attempts - returned from the bus stop, returned from the corner shop, returned from the bridge over the canal, thrown by Andrew Snell into the same canal. He believed it to be bullying, she wanted to kiss him with gratitude.

Left Foot

1. Her flat stomach, lost slowly, gradually. Baby 1, baby 2, a weakness for chocolate biscuits eaten noiselessly straight from the packet. Middle age, middle spread. She misses the taut flesh, but not enough to do anything about it.

2. A black thong, expensive, lacey, frivolous, worn for the man who gave her the key, also lost. For weeks afterwards, she tortured herself, imagining the underwear dropped from her bag in front of a colleague, a

neighbor, her husband. She examined faces for knowing expressions, but nothing changed and finally she relaxed.
Felt safe.

3. The collected poems of Sylvia Plath - Shunted from bag to bag, dependent on her outfit, a talisman against boredom in the days before touch screens and I- things. She considered buying another copy but found herself satisfied with "Take a Break" and "Hello" magazines.

4. A job, one to which she was so unsuited that she expected to lose it every day, practiced appropriate expressions of regret, dismay, made sure that she kept nothing important, irreplaceable in her desk draws, just in case. The actual loss was something of an anti-climax after all.

5. Her virginity, it weighed heavily on her 16-year-old self and she gave it up happily to Nigel, he of the moped and the racing green hand knitted jumper. In retrospect, she wonders if he also lost his virgin status during their inept fumbling's in his mothers' bed.

Right Foot

[Getting tougher now, but sleep feels nearer now, mustn't stop now]

1. A breast and appropriately a right breast, enumerated on this right foot. She thought she would miss it more than she did, but by the time it went, she could look at it only with loathing, betrayer, mutant, mutating. No real loss at all.

2. Her youth, it seemed to leave her in one single day. She went to bed and woke, middle aged, as if the fairies had stolen it while she slept. She searches for it, in mirrors, in perfumed pots and jars. It has remained, defiantly lost.

3. Hope, its loss etched on her lips, permanently downward turning now, even when she smiles. The ghost of loss bleeding through.

4. A lost child, birthday still remembered but distantly, maths needed to work out the date. Sometimes overlooked until the day is half, two thirds, three quarters done, but then recalled, the day paused and then the memory put away for another year.

[Stop, stop now, focus on the last toe, the smallest, nail painted, soft pink - an easy loss, nothing loss]

5. A five-pound note, a small amount, inconsiderable, unimportant, perhaps not lost at all, perhaps put away, hidden, safe against a rainy day.

Grim Little Things

Grim

Little

Things

Snail slime tracking across the pillow,
heading not towards the windowsill and away,
but downwards, towards the tangle of duvet and
sheets.

That moment, with eyes still half closed,
you swing your feet out of bed and your toes find
something wet, soft and still just slightly warm.

Sniffing milk to test for freshness,
the almost solidity of turn, throat gagging on smell
alone.

The crowded bus, the man too close,
stale sweat imperfectly masked by cheap deodorant,
his (at least to you) unwelcome erection jabs against
your hip at every speed bump.

The way a colleague chews her lunch,
mouth open, a whale seeking krill
and all the time you cannot tear your eyes away,
mastication and conversation.

A used dressing, plaster, still damp,

sticky, viscous and dropped by some stranger into your wheelie bin.

A lipstick left, inadvertently, to melt on a sunny windowsill.

A bloodied thumb print, just the one, off centre on a downstairs light switch.

Chickens, necks yellowed, hanging by their greying feet in the make-shift Halal butchers' storefront.

A toenail, blackened, hanging by a single thread, walking, you feel it move, shift under woollen socks, but fear the final loss, the display of pink unready flesh.

Coppers sticky from over handling pressed into your hand in part payment for 10 cut price cigarettes.

A windscreen splattered, with the flying dead and the noise the wipers make removing the crispy bits.

Under-cooked quiche, onion floating in a thin soup of egginess.

A pug, eyes a popping, pink onesie and a matching pink collar.

Knuckles cracking, slow, deliberate, preparation and then the silence.

That Nokia ringtone
Da da da ..dadad da....dada da da.

Any brown envelope with any Government dept
stamp.

Cells mutating under a microscope.

An ageing neck.

And on
and on and
on and on

Why I Ran Away...Voices of The Disappeared

One day I ran away to join the circus, but that there wasn't any circus, so I just ran away instead.

I didn't come off the motorway at the usual exit, I just kept driving until I ran out of petrol and then I sat in the car with my head on the steering wheel while I waited for something to happen.

Before I walked away, I cleaned the bathroom, even the bits that didn't show, I knew that everyone would think badly enough of me, I didn't want them to think I was dirty too.

I sat at work, adding up figures and suddenly realised that I hadn't managed one act of significance in my life.

I ran before it all came crashing down, the sense of relief was immense.

I couldn't bear the way she looked at me, couldn't bear the way she tried to keep the children quiet, convinced myself that they would all be better off if I wasn't there.

I tried to pretend that nothing had changed, that I was still the same person. On the nights when I woke, covered in sweat, my wife cowering in a corner of the bedroom, keeping that pretence going seemed impossible.

I couldn't get her to shut up, couldn't stop her asking for more and more. I walked out early one morning.

I didn't look back.

I ran away the day before the building society repossessed the house.

I walked out of my life and nobody noticed.

He broke my heart and made a mockery of my carefully constructed little life, so I went in search of a better one.

When I lost my job, I knew I should go home to face the music, but I caught a train instead.

I realised that I only stayed to give the dog a home, so I left and took the dog with me.

The more I owned, the more it all seemed a burden, I dreamt of being weightless, so I took the smallest bag we had and even that seemed too much to own.

I wanted less history, to be someone different , to reinvent myself. I sat on a bus, considering and discarding new first names.

I wanted someone to miss me.

I couldn't find a way of going back, so I didn't, but I wish I could, sometimes.

I ran away because I was too afraid to stay.

About The Author

Cathi Rae is a poet and spoken word artist, somewhat accidentally living in the Midlands. After a long career in education, she now earns her living cleaning other people's houses, which is a walk in the park after decades in the salt mines of learning.

She generally prefers dogs to people and is living proof that it can take a really long time to work out what you actually want to do with your life.

She is currently studying for an MA in creative writing at Leicester University.

Printed in Great Britain
by Amazon

84127540R00061